W9-APR-832

The new Solar System
System
Stars

Robin Birch

CHELSEA CLUBHOUSE
An Imprint of Chelsea House Publishers

This edition published in 2008 in the United States of America by Chelsea Clubhouse, a division of Chelsea House Publishers.

Chelsea Clubhouse
An imprint of Chelsea House Publishers
132 West 31st Street
New York, NY 10001

Chelsea Clubhouse books are available at special discounts when purchased in bulk quantities for businesses, associations, institutions, or sales promotions. Please call our Special Sales Department in New York at (212) 967-8800 or (800) 322-8755.

You can find Chelsea Clubhouse on the World Wide Web at: http://www.chelseahouse.com

First published in 2004 by
MACMILLAN EDUCATION AUSTRALIA PTY LTD
15–19 Claremont Street, South Yarra, 3141

Visit our Web site at www.macmillan.com.au or go directly to www.macmillanlibrary.com.au

Associated companies and representatives throughout the world.

Library of Congress Cataloging-in-Publication Data

Birch, Robin.
  Stars / Robin Birch.
  p. cm. — (New solar system)
  Includes index.
  ISBN 978-1-60413-206-9
  1. Stars—Juvenile literature. I. Title.
  QB801.7.B57 2008
  523.8—dc22

2007051332

Edited by Anna Fern
Text and cover design by Cristina Neri, Canary Graphic Design
Photo research by Legend Images
Illustrations by Melissa Webb, Noisypics

Printed in the United States of America

Acknowledgements

The author and publisher are grateful to the following for permission to reproduce copyright material:

Cover photograph of stars courtesy of Photodisc.

Scott Camazine—OSF/Auscape, p. 4; J. P. Lescourret—Explorer/Auscape, p. 5 (top); TSADO/NASA/Tom Stack/Auscape, p. 26 (bottom); Australian Picture Library/Corbis, p. 6 (top); Digital Vision, p. 10; Calvin J. Hamilton, p. 17; NASA/Caltech, p. 27 (bottom); NASA/JPL, p. 26 (top); Photodisc, pp. 8 (top), 23 (top left), 28 (top right & bottom), 29 (all); Photolibrary.com/SPL, pp. 6 (bottom), 8 (bottom), 9, 16, 18, 19, 20, 21, 22, 23 (top right), 24, 25, 27 (top), 28 (top left).

Background and border images courtesy of Photodisc.

Please note
At the time of printing, the Internet addresses appearing in this book were correct. Owing to the dynamic nature of the Internet, however, we cannot guarantee that all these addresses will remain correct.

Contents

Glossary words

When you see a word printed in bold, **like this**, you can look up its meaning in the glossary on page 31.

The Night Sky

Stars are huge, glowing balls of **gas**. They look tiny because they are a long way away.

On a clear night, we can see up to 3,000 stars. If we look carefully, we can see that stars are different colors. They may be white, yellow-white, orange-white, or blue-white. The colors can help us figure out how large and how old stars are.

Stars have tiny points of light coming from them which move around. This effect is called "twinkling." Twinkling is caused by Earth's **atmosphere**. The atmosphere is moving around, so it makes the starlight move around.

▼ Some stars, such as the Pleiades cluster, are grouped together. This happens where several stars have formed together at around the same time.

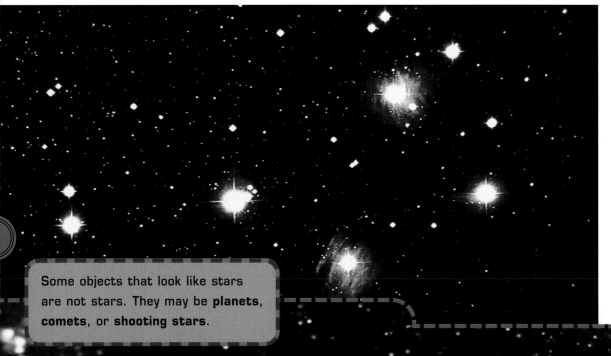

Some objects that look like stars are not stars. They may be **planets**, **comets**, or **shooting stars**.

◀ The pyramids, in Egypt, pointed the way to certain stars.

In **ancient** times, many people thought that the sky was either a flat or domed roof over Earth, with the stars attached to it.

Ancient Babylonian and Chinese people worked out calendars based on movements of the stars. The Egyptians made star maps and built pyramids that showed the way to certain stars, to help the dead in the afterlife.

Ancient people saw patterns made by the stars in the shapes of people and animals. They used these patterns to tell stories which were important to them.

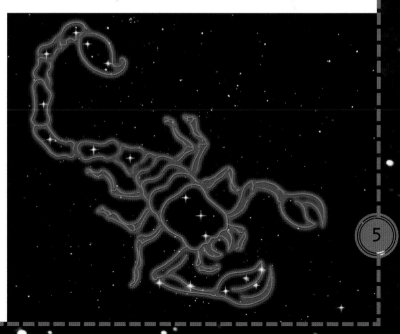

▶ Scorpius the scorpion. In very old stories, Scorpius had a fight with Orion the hunter and killed him. He was sent to the opposite side of the sky as punishment.

Watching Stars

Stars can be seen best when there is no Moon or human-made light in the sky. **Binoculars** are good for looking at some objects, as long as you know exactly where to look. Binoculars make objects look more detailed.

▲ Using binoculars

Sirius

▲ Sirius is the brightest star in the sky.

Light Years

Stars are such a long way away from us that it becomes difficult to state the distances in miles or kilometers. It is easier to state the distances of stars in light years. One light year is the distance that light travels in one year.

The star Sirius is 8.6 light years away from Earth. When we look at Sirius, we are seeing how it looked 8.6 years ago.

Light travels at a speed of 186,000 miles (300,000 kilometers) per second. One light year is a distance of about 5,900,000,000,000 miles (9,500,000,000,000 kilometers).

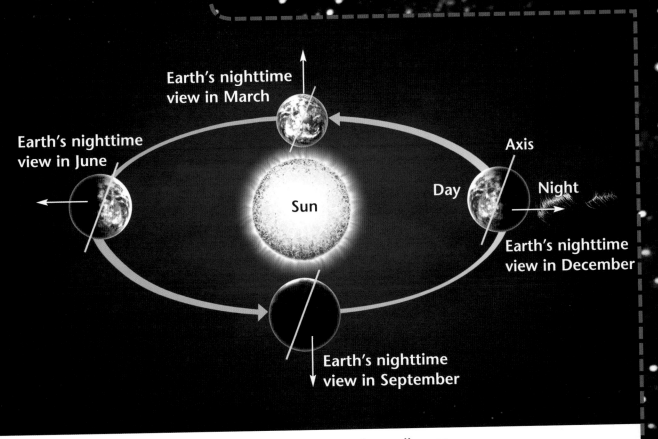

Earth's nighttime view in March

Earth's nighttime view in June

Sun

Axis

Day

Night

Earth's nighttime view in December

Earth's nighttime view in September

▲ People on Earth see different stars, depending on where Earth is in its journey around the Sun.

Changing Views

Earth **rotates** on its **axis** once every 24 hours. Because of this, the stars move slowly across the sky during the night, mainly from east to west. The stars are not really moving. It is we, on Earth, who are moving.

Different stars can be seen in the sky at different times of the year. This is because we see into different parts of space as Earth **orbits** the Sun. The stars are all around Earth and the Sun, but they are a long distance away. We only see stars at night, because the Sun is too bright to see them during the day.

The Milky Way

On a very dark, clear night in a dark area, stars can be seen shining very brightly. Most of the stars are seen as definite pinpoints of light. A narrow cloud, which looks similar to a rain cloud, can also be seen stretching right across the sky. This is a cloud of very faint stars, called the Milky Way. It was called this because it looks like milk has been spilt across the sky.

◀ A spiral galaxy

Galaxies

Galaxies are huge groups of stars which can have up to 3,000 **billion** stars in them. There are several types of galaxies, of different sizes and shapes. Billions of galaxies have been found in space. The Milky Way that we see in the sky is part of the galaxy called the Milky Way galaxy.

▶ The Sombrero galaxy

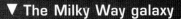

Milky Way Galaxy and the Solar System

The Milky Way galaxy is round and flat, like a flying saucer. It is wider in the middle than on the outside and has a spiral shape. The Milky Way contains about 200 billion stars.

The **solar system** is in the Milky Way galaxy. The Sun is a star in one of the arms of the Milky Way galaxy, towards the outside of the galaxy. The Sun is slowly orbiting the center of the Milky Way galaxy. It slowly passes through the arms, and then the area between the arms. It takes the Sun about 220 million years to circle the Milky Way once.

What Is a Star?

A star is a huge ball of glowing gas.

Star Formation

A star forms in an enormous cloud of gas which is floating in space. This gas cloud is called a nebula. A nebula is made mostly of the substance hydrogen.

A star begins forming when gas in a nebula starts swirling around more than usual. The gas particles bump into each other and heat up. The gas forms a tight ball and heats up even more. When the gas reaches a temperature of 18 million degrees Fahrenheit (10 million degrees Celsius), nuclear fusion starts in the **core** of the ball. When nuclear fusion starts, the hot ball of gas becomes a star.

Nuclear fusion is a process where hydrogen particles join together to make particles of the substance helium. When this happens, huge amounts of heat and light energy are given off.

▶ Nebula containing young stars

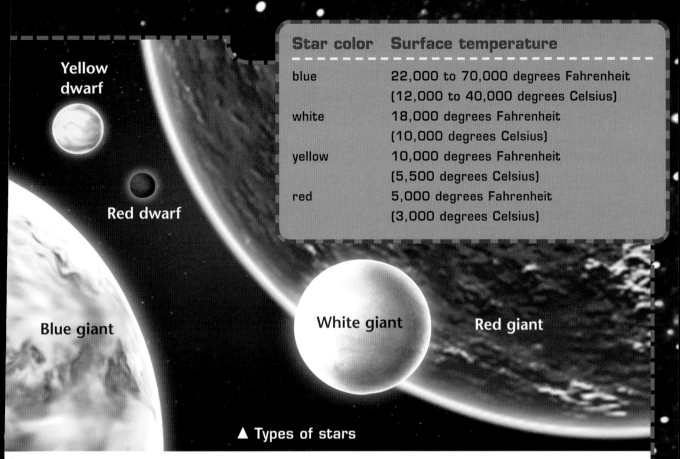

Star color	Surface temperature
blue	22,000 to 70,000 degrees Fahrenheit
	(12,000 to 40,000 degrees Celsius)
white	18,000 degrees Fahrenheit
	(10,000 degrees Celsius)
yellow	10,000 degrees Fahrenheit
	(5,500 degrees Celsius)
red	5,000 degrees Fahrenheit
	(3,000 degrees Celsius)

Yellow dwarf

Red dwarf

Blue giant

White giant

Red giant

▲ Types of stars

Types of Stars

Stars are different sizes, temperatures, and colors. Young stars are larger when they have more gas in them.

The color of a star depends on the temperature of its outside surface.

- The largest young stars are the hottest, and they are blue. They are called blue giants and blue supergiants.
- The next largest and hottest young stars are white, and then yellow. These stars are called white giants and yellow dwarves.
- The smallest of the young stars are the coolest. These stars are red, and they are called red dwarves.

When stars get old, they expand. The outside surface cools down and turns red. These stars are called red giants and red supergiants.

Star Death

Old stars expand and become red giants and red supergiants. This happens when the hydrogen gas in their cores runs out. Then nuclear fusion in the cores stops.

Smaller red giants eventually collapse. The outer layers of gas in the red giant are thrown outwards, making a ring around the core of the red giant. The gas, or nebula, then drifts away.

The core of the red giant collapses further and becomes an object called a white dwarf. A white dwarf is about the size of Earth. White dwarves shine brightly, but they do not have nuclear fusion going on inside them. Then they fade to become a dead, black object floating in space.

▼ Death of a smaller red giant

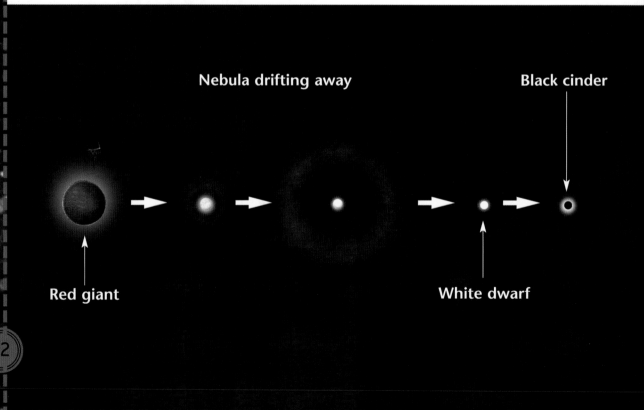

Nebula drifting away

Black cinder

Red giant

White dwarf

Red giant

Neutron star

Supernova

▲ Death of a larger red giant

Larger red giants eventually explode. The huge ball of exploding gas is called a nova or supernova. These explosions look like new, bright stars and can last for a few months. Astronomers find several of these explosions every year, with **telescopes**.

The outer layers of the nova or supernova drift away and make a new nebula, floating in space. The core contracts very tightly and becomes a neutron star.

Some neutron stars give off bursts of **radio signals** as they spin. These stars are called pulsars. Other neutron stars keep contracting, until they become very **dense**. If they become dense enough, these stars become black holes.

The Sun

The Sun is a yellow dwarf star. Even though it is called a dwarf, the Sun is bigger than most stars. Some stars are many times bigger than the Sun, however.

The Sun's **diameter** is 863,000 miles (1,390,000 kilometers). This is about 109 times the diameter of Earth. Its outside surface temperature is about 9,900 degrees Fahrenheit (5,500 degrees Celsius). The temperature of the core is about 27,000,000 degrees Fahrenheit (15,000,000 degrees Celsius). The Sun today is made of about 75 percent hydrogen and about 25 percent helium.

The Sun became a star about 4,600 million years ago. It will probably go on shining for another 5,000 million years without changing much. In that time, it will probably become a little larger and a little brighter.

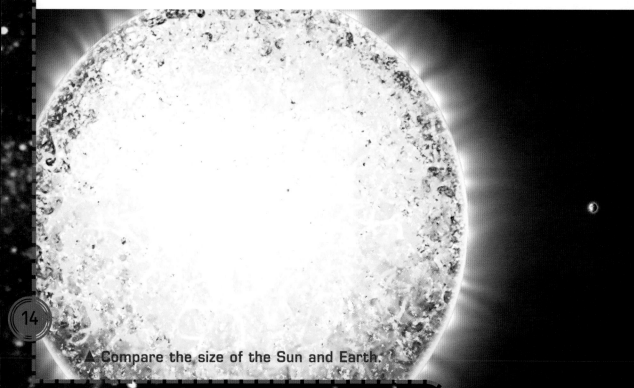

▲ Compare the size of the Sun and Earth.

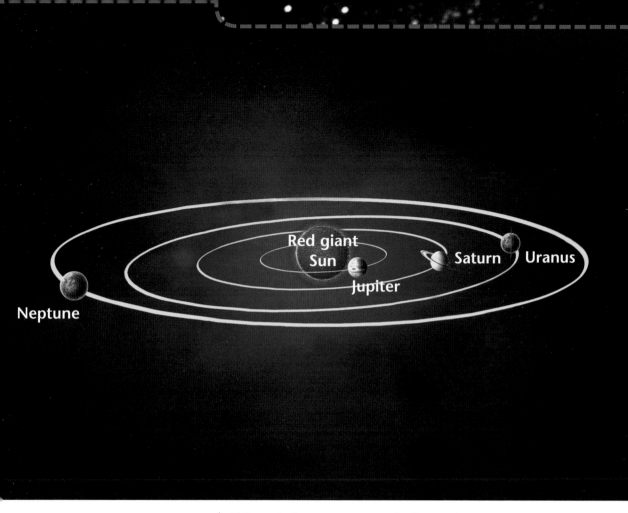

Red giant
Sun

Jupiter

Saturn   Uranus

Neptune

▲ When it becomes a red giant, the Sun will
swallow up the inner planets.

Death of the Sun

In about 5,000 million years from now, the Sun will probably expand fairly quickly and become a red giant. When the Sun is a red giant, it will probably be so large that it will swallow up Earth. The Sun will probably last about 1,000 million years as a red giant.

The red giant Sun will finally collapse and its outer layers of gas will be thrown off into space. The core of the Sun will become a white dwarf.

The Solar System

The Sun has many bodies revolving around it. The Sun and the other bodies all formed in the same nebula, about 4,600 million years ago. The Sun and these bodies together are called the solar system.

The solar system has eight planets. Mercury, Venus, Earth, and Mars are made of rock. They are the smallest planets, and are closest to the Sun. Jupiter, Saturn, Uranus, and Neptune are made mainly of gas and liquid. They are the largest planets, and are farthest from the Sun.

The solar system also has dwarf planets. The first three bodies to be called dwarf planets were Ceres, Pluto, and Eris. Ceres is an asteroid. Pluto and Eris are known as **trans-Neptunian objects**.

A planet is a body that:

- orbits the Sun
- is nearly round in shape
- has cleared the area around its orbit (its **gravity** is strong enough)

A dwarf planet is a body that:

- orbits the Sun
- is nearly round in shape
- has not cleared the area around its orbit
- is not a **moon**

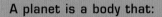

▲ The solar system

Planet	Average distance from Sun	
Mercury	35,960,000 miles	(57,910,000 kilometers)
Venus	67,190,000 miles	(108,200,000 kilometers)
Earth	92,900,000 miles	(149,600,000 kilometers)
Mars	141,550,000 miles	(227,940,000 kilometers)
Jupiter	483,340,000 miles	(778,330,000 kilometers)
Saturn	887,660,000 miles	(1,429,400,000 kilometers)
Uranus	1,782,880,000 miles	(2,870,990,000 kilometers)
Neptune	2,796,000,000 miles	(4,504,000,000 kilometers)

The name "solar system" comes from the word "Sol," the Latin name for the Sun.

▶ The eight planets are Mercury, Venus, Earth, Mars, Jupiter, Saturn, Uranus, and Neptune.

The solar system is about 4,600 million years old.

There are also many small solar-system bodies in the solar system. They include any asteroids, comets, trans-Neptunian objects, or other small bodies that have not been called dwarf planets.

Asteroids are made of rock. Most of them, including dwarf planet Ceres, orbit the Sun in a path called the asteroid belt. The asteroid belt lies between the orbits of Mars and Jupiter. Comets are made mainly of ice and rock. When their orbits bring them close to the Sun, comets grow a tail. Trans-Neptunian objects are icy, and orbit the Sun farther out on average than Neptune.

Constellations

Constellations are groups of stars in certain areas of the sky. Often these groups of stars make patterns which people recognize.

People have told many stories about the people, animals, and objects they have seen in the patterns of stars. Today astronomers have divided the sky into 88 constellations, which are named in the Latin language.

People in the Northern **Hemisphere** see many different stars from people in the Southern Hemisphere. Other stars are seen by people in both the Northern and Southern hemispheres.

▲ Sagittarius, the archer, is a constellation.

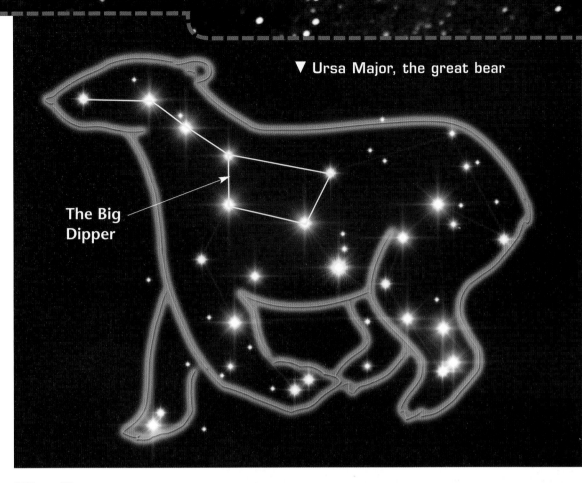

▼ Ursa Major, the great bear

The Big Dipper

The Bears

People in the Northern Hemisphere see two famous constellations. One is called Ursa Major, the great bear. The other is called Ursa Minor, the smaller bear.

Ursa Major, the great bear, has some very bright stars which people know well. These stars are often called the "Big Dipper" because they look like a dipper, which is used for carrying water. The Big Dipper looks like a saucepan with a long handle.

Ursa Minor, the smaller bear, only has two bright stars. One of these bright stars is right above Earth's North **Pole**, and does not move during the night. This star is called Polaris, or the North Star. The North Star is in an exact north direction and was used by sailors at sea to find north.

Southern Cross

People in the Southern Hemisphere see the constellation Crux.
This constellation is commonly called the "Southern Cross."
The Southern Cross has four bright stars shaped like a cross or
a kite. The brightest star is really two blue stars close together.

There are two stars near the Southern Cross which point at
one end of the cross shape. These two stars are known as the
Pointers. One of the Pointers is called Alpha Centauri. This star
is the closest star to the Sun. Alpha Centauri is 4.3 light years
away from Earth and the Sun.

▼The Southern Cross

People who lived in
the Pacific Ocean
area used the
Southern Cross to
find their way at
sea. They knew that
when the Southern
Cross was upright,
it was pointing
exactly south.

The ancient Egyptians used Sirius to tell them when the Nile River would flood. They knew that when Sirius was seen rising in the first rays of sunrise, the Nile would soon flood.

The Great Dog

People on most parts of Earth can see the constellation Canis Major, the great dog. The brightest stars of Canis Major make the dog's neck, back, tail, a front leg, and a back leg.

Sirius is the brightest star in Canis Major and the brightest star in the sky. It is at the neck of the dog. Sirius is really a double star. It is a large blue-white star with a white dwarf circling around it.

Near Canis Major is another dog constellation called Canis Minor, the smaller dog. Canis Minor has only one bright star.

Orion, the Hunter

People on most parts of Earth can see the constellation Orion, the hunter. The brightest stars of Orion make the hunter's shoulders, belt, sword, a knee, and a foot. He is usually shown carrying a club and a lion's skin.

One of Orion's bright shoulder stars is called Betelgeuse. Betelgeuse is a red giant star. The bright star which makes one of Orion's feet is called Rigel. Rigel is a blue giant star. The colors of Betelgeuse and Rigel are easy to see.

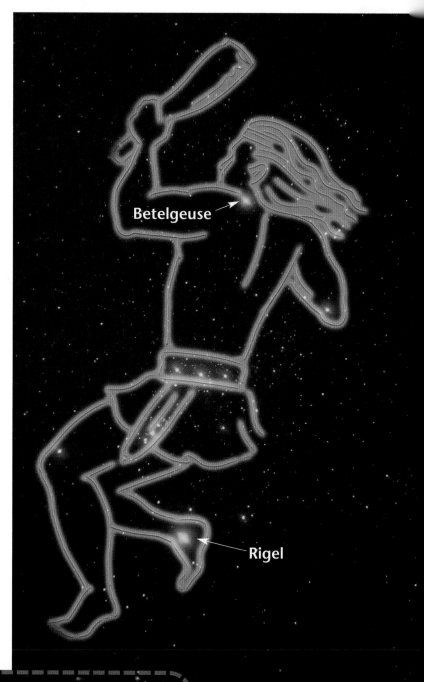

Betelgeuse

Rigel

▶ Orion, the hunter

▲ The Great Nebula in Orion

▶ The Horsehead Nebula

Orion's sword has three stars in it. The middle star is really stars in a nebula. This nebula is called the Great Nebula in Orion. There is also a nebula near Orion's belt, called the Horsehead Nebula. A nebula is a cloud of gas and dust. Stars are formed in nebulas.

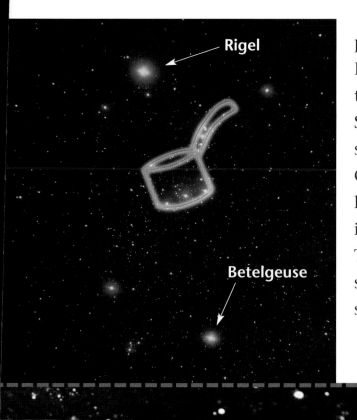

Rigel

Betelgeuse

◀ The saucepan

Orion was named by people in the Northern Hemisphere, who see Orion the right way up. In the Southern Hemisphere, people see Orion upside-down. Orion's belt and sword look like a large saucepan to people in the Southern Hemisphere. The belt is the bottom of the saucepan, and the sword is the saucepan's handle.

The Zodiac

The pattern the stars make in the sky stays the same. It does not change from month to month or year to year. When the stars move through the sky, the whole star pattern moves together.

The planets, Moon, and Sun change their positions compared to the stars around them. The word "planet" means "wanderer." Early people gave planets this name because they noticed the planets wandered around the star patterns.

The planets, Moon, and Sun always wander across the same constellations in the sky. These constellations form a band across the sky, going from west to east. The constellations form the zodiac.

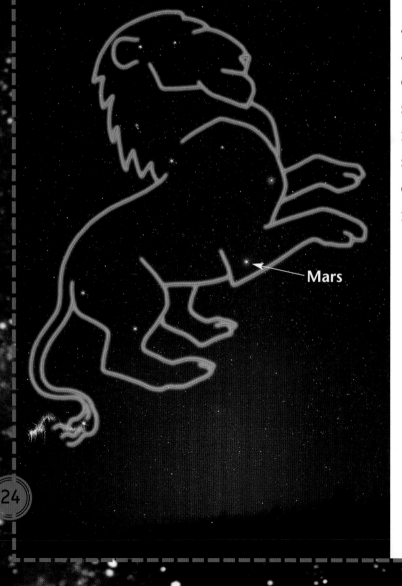
Mars

◀ Mars in Leo, the lion

▲ Taurus the Bull

The zodiac today has 13 constellations. When ancient people started observing the zodiac, Earth was facing in a slightly different direction into space from where it is now, and the zodiac position has changed a little. Ancient people decided on 12 zodiac constellations, and these are the ones that most people know today.

The 12 **traditional** zodiac constellations are:

- Aries
- Taurus
- Gemini
- Cancer
- Leo
- Virgo
- Libra
- Scorpio
- Sagittarius
- Capricorn
- Aquarius
- Pisces

The planets, Moon, and Sun move across them in this order. The thirteenth constellation is Ophiuchus, which is between Scorpio and Sagittarius.

Studying Stars

Stars give off light rays. They also give off gamma rays, X rays, ultraviolet rays, infrared rays, and radio waves. Astronomers use instruments to collect all of these types of rays to learn about stars.

Satellites

Satellites orbiting Earth pick up rays which cannot pass through Earth's atmosphere. They beam the information they collect back to astronomers on Earth. These rays are the gamma rays, X rays, most ultraviolet rays, and some infrared rays. Telescopes on Earth pick up light rays, infrared rays, and radio waves.

▲ An artist's impression of a space telescope's infrared view of the Milky Way galaxy.

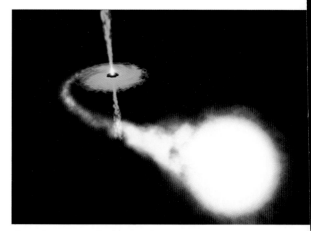

▲ X rays provided the information to make this picture of energy around a black hole.

26

Dust clouds in space often block the view of stars from Earth. These stars can be detected by collecting their infrared rays.

▶ An example of a star spectrum

Spectrometers

When it shines though a prism, such as a piece of cut glass, light breaks up into rainbow colors, called a spectrum. Astronomers use instruments called spectrometers to break starlight up into rainbow colors. Star **spectra** have lots of thin, black lines across them. The lines tell astronomers what substances are in the stars.

The positions of the black lines on star spectra can also tell astronomers how fast a star is moving, and whether it is moving away from us or towards us. By looking at spectra, astronomers have discovered that all distant galaxies are moving away from us. We could say that, because of this, the **universe** is expanding.

▼ Distant galaxies—the brightest and nearest are in blue, and the faintest, most distant ones are in red.

Telescopes on Earth

On land, astronomers use optical telescopes, which make things look larger and more detailed. These telescopes collect light rays and infrared rays. The rays pass through lenses and are usually reflected by mirrors in these telescopes. The rays are focused, making an image, and often photographed. Large telescopes of this type are usually built in places with clear skies, away from cities and towns.

▲ An optical telescope

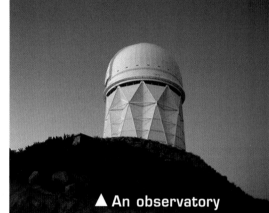

▲ An observatory

Radio telescopes are used to collect radio waves. They have large dish-shaped antennas for collecting the radio waves. Some radio telescopes have several dishes on train tracks so they can be spread over a wide area. This is like having one very big dish. This type of radio telescope is called an array.

▼ Radio telescope array

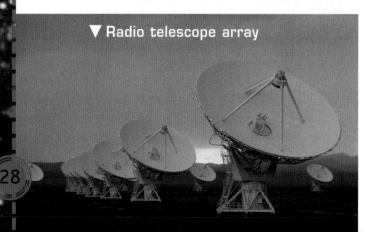

The *HST* photographed this cloud of hydrogen gas and dust 7,000 light years away from Earth. It is part of the Eagle Nebula, which glows from very young stars inside it.

▼ This cloud of gas, 8,000 light years away from Earth, was photographed by the *HST*. It is a star which is dying, and throwing off gas.

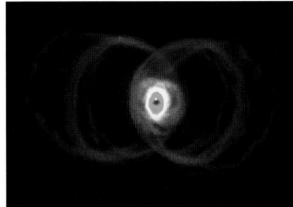

Hubble Space Telescope

The *Hubble Space Telescope* (*HST*) orbits Earth above the atmosphere, in space. It can detect rays which are blocked by the atmosphere. The *HST* has cameras and spectrometers on board, and it collects light rays and infrared rays. It beams the information it gathers back to astronomers on Earth.

The *HST* has discovered new stars, nebulas, and galaxies. It has shown astronomers objects which are much farther away than they had seen before.

▼ The *Hubble Space Telescope* above Earth

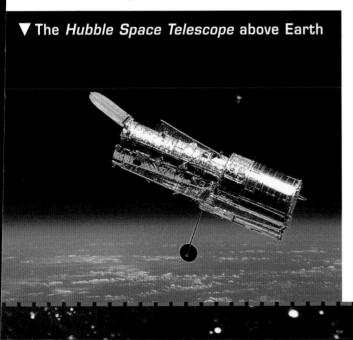

29

Star Fact Summary

Stars are made of	mainly hydrogen gas
Star sizes	thousands of miles to hundreds of millions of miles across
Star colors	red, orange, yellow, white, blue
Star surface temperatures	5,000 to 70,000 degrees Fahrenheit (3,000 to 40,000 degrees Celsius)
Light year	5,900,000,000,000 miles (9,500,000,000,000 kilometers)
12 brightest stars	Sun, Sirius, Canopus, Alpha Centauri, Arcturus, Vega, Capella, Rigel, Procyan, Achernar, Betelgeuse, Hadar

Web Sites

www.enchantedlearning.com
Enchanted Learning Web site—click on "Astronomy"

stardate.org
Stargazing with the University of Texas McDonald Observatory

hubblesite.org
The *Hubble Space Telescope*

nssdc.gsfc.nasa.gov/photo_gallery/
Photo gallery of the NASA National Space Science Data Center

Glossary

ancient lived thousands of years ago

astronomers people who study stars, planets, and other bodies in space

atmosphere a layer of gas around a large body in space

axis an imaginary line through the middle of an object, from top to bottom

billion 1,000 million

binoculars an instrument with two eye pieces, for making faraway objects look bigger and more detailed

comets large balls of rock, ice, gas, and dust which orbit the Sun

core the center, or middle part of a solar system body

dense heavy for its size

diameter the distance across

gas a substance in which the particles are far apart, not solid or liquid

gravity a force which pulls one body towards another body

hemisphere half of a globe

moon a natural body which circles around a planet or other body

orbits travels on a path around another body in space

pole the top or bottom of a globe

radio signals invisible rays

rotates spins

satellites natural or human-made objects which revolve around another body

shooting stars rocks and dust burning up as they fall through the atmosphere

solar system the Sun and the bodies which circle around it

spectra more than one spectrum

telescopes instruments for making faraway objects look bigger and more detailed

traditional known about by lots of people for a long time

trans-Neptunian objects small solar system bodies which orbit the Sun farther out than Neptune, on average

universe all of space

Index